CHARACTERISTICS OF THE AGE:

A DISCOURSE

DELIVERED

IN THE FIRST PRESBYTERIAN CHURCH,

TROY, N. Y.,

ON THANKSGIVING DAY,

DECEMBER 12, 1850,

BY NATHAN S. S. BEMAN, D. D.

TROY, N. Y.:
YOUNG AND HARTT, 216 RIVER STREET.
1851.

TROY DAILY WHIG PRINT.

CORRESPONDENCE.

TROY, DECEMBER 13, 1850.

Rev. N. S. S. Beman, D. D.:

DEAR SIR,

We are earnestly solicited by many of our fellow-citizens to request of you, for publication, a copy of your THANKSGIVING DISCOURSE. Its comprehensive, patriotic, and law-abiding sentiments demand a wide diffusion, and lead us cordially to unite in the wish generally expressed by your intelligent auditors, to publish the same.

Very respectfully,

Your obedient servants,

STEPHEN WICKES,	PLINY A. MOORE,	*Trustees, &c.*
JOHN FREEMAN,	BENJ. HATCH,	
DAVID COWEE,	JAMES H. HOWE,	

A similar request has been made, in a respectful Letter addressed to me, by the following gentlemen: HIRAM SLOCUM, WM. F. SAGE, JOB S. OLIN, A. F. WHEELER, J. VAN SCHOONHOVEN, L. FAIRBANKS, Jr., G. ROBERTSON, Jr., GILES B. KELLOGG, MARTIN I. TOWNSEND, and F. S. THAYER, Esquires.

To the Trustees, and other Gentlemen:

Permit me, in one word, to say I cannot but be highly gratified by your request for a copy of my Discourse for the press. The manuscript is at your disposal.

Most truly yours,

N. S. S. BEMAN.

TROY, DECEMBER 14, 1850.

CHARACTERISTICS OF THE AGE.

"For verily I say unto you, that many prophets and righteous men have desired to see those things which ye see, and have not seen them; and to hear those things which ye hear, and have not heard them."—MAT. XIII. 17.

WE have assembled this morning in compliance with one of the time-honored customs of our own country. The practice of observing a day of annual Thanksgiving, originated in New England, among the early colonists, who have generally been denominated Puritans. They rejected all traditions and all human authority in matters of religion, and professed to take the Scriptures as their only and sufficient guide. In carrying out this principle, they refused to observe those numerous Festivals, called "Holy Days," which had been introduced by the Roman hierarchy, and perpetuated by the various church-establishments of Europe, and which had been enjoined on the people, by human legislation, as a part of the religion of Jesus Christ and his apostles, taught in the gospel.

But notwithstanding this disregard of many of the popular forms of christianity, which they believed were really the inventions of men, no people in the world were more scrupulous in their regard for the externals of religion. The

Sabbath and Sanctuary were embalmed in their hearts. The whole population seemed to feel their heavenly influence. With them religion was an inward principle and an outward life. In conformity with this character, they early set apart, by conventional agreement, and not by ecclesiastical authority, nor as a matter of church order, two days in the year, as convenience, from time to time, might dictate, for the voluntary offerings of a people in the full enjoyment of religious liberty. In the Spring, when the rugged features of winter began to relax into genial smiles, and the earth was unbound from its icy fetters, and invited the husbandman forth with his plow and spade, as preparatory to the seed-corn now to be deposited in hope, they sought the blessing of God in public "*humiliation, fasting and prayer;*" and in the Autumn, when the ripe fruits were gathered into their barns, garners, and other storehouses, they proclaimed and observed a day of public "Thanksgiving," in grateful remembrance of the goodness of God which had crowned the year. This custom has been gradually gaining ground in our republic, and seems destined ultimately to find a place in the religious sympathies of all the States of the Union.

Topics of discussion, without number, present themselves on such an occasion, and solicit our attention. I might remind you of your rank among the creatures of God, "made a little lower than the angels,"—of your birth-right as Americans, occupying the fairest portion of God's universal heritage,—of the institutions of Government and learning which distinguish our country, in many respects, from all others,—of our entire religious freedom, having nothing to fear from the Bulls of Popes, or the decrees of Councils, or the legislation of political religionists,—of the peculiar success of an untrammelled gospel among our own people,—of christian churches, scattered over our own land, having, with a few rare exceptions, no tendency towards the mother of abominations,—of the extent, resources, prosperity and growing intelligence of our own Empire State,—of the triumph of principle in favor of popular education, in the late vote sustaining the Free-School system,—of our peculiar exemption from the blue scourge of pestilence, during the last year,—of the luxuriant productions of our harvest-fields,—of the blessings of sweet peace which pervade all our borders,—of the preservation of the union of the States, amid the conflicts of sectional interests and the storms of heated passion,—of the national strength and glory which we may hope for in the future,—of our individual benefactions from heaven, which every man can recount for himself,—of God's gift of the Bible which we hold in our hands,—and of the hope of future glory which we may cherish through Jesus Christ: and in recounting these benefactions, I might emphatically call upon each individual before me to adopt the language of the Psalmist;—"Bless the Lord, O my soul, and forget not all his benefits." But I shall pass by all these, though quite natural, and appropriate to the occasion, to consider a single one suggested by the words of my text. "For verily I say unto you, that many prophets and righteous men have desired to see those things which ye see, and have not seen them; and to hear those things which ye hear, and have not heard them."

The sentiment here expressed, is this,—that the disciples whom Christ addressed should be thankful for what they were permitted *to see and hear.* Many had desired these blessings, but had not enjoyed them. Other ages had been characterized by promise and expectation; in that age, promise was fulfilled, and expectation gratified. The particular event referred to was the consummation of prophesy, in the Mission of Christ That result they witnessed, and they might well be thankful that they were permitted to live in that age.

So it may be said of *ourselves*. We live in an age of grand results. These have been anticipated, and looked for, and longed for,—but many generations have "died without the sight." 'Our eyes see, and our ears hear.' Our age is full of magnificent events; and we should be thankful that we live in such an era. "For verily I say unto you, that many prophets and righteous men have desired to see those things which ye see, and have not seen them; and to hear those things which ye hear, and have not heard them." My subject, is, the characteristics of the age in which we live.

THE CHARACTERISTICS OF THE PRESENT AGE.

1. Our age is characterized *by the practical results of science.*

The day in which we live is more distinguished for inventions than discoveries. Indeed, this is the usual order of human progress. Discoveries are prior in their existence to inventions, because the former may be considered, in some sense, the parents of the latter. A discovery consists in bringing to light some hidden fact or principle which has had a previous existence, and which has not been before observed or known by men. An invention is the application of this discovery to some new, and, generally, to some useful purpose. The polarity of the magnet has always existed as a fact of nature, but the knowledge of this fact was an important discovery which resulted from human research. The application of this newly developed principle of nature to the mariner's compass—by the aid of which, unknown and trackless seas are traversed, and the globe we inhabit circumnavigated with almost unerring exactitude—is an invention of human genius, by which the whole face of our world has been changed.

Our age is one of utility. Principles which have long since been discovered and investigated, by minds of deep research, and which have been taught and contemplated only in theory and speculation, are now eagerly seized upon and applied to the practical purposes of life. The elasticity of *steam* has been observed and experimented upon by scientific men, with a view to its employment as a useful agent, for two centuries and a half; but it was reserved for our day to witness the application of this power to a greater variety of important practical purposes, perhaps, than any other agent in nature. In the successive appropriations of this old and long-dormant power, we have seen the beautiful and majestic steamer gliding with celerity along our navigable rivers, against wind and stream and tide; and then the ocean-ship, under the same impulse, holding on her stately and steady course, in defiance of the stiff breeze and adverse currents, and in conscious fearlessness of the warring elements which upturn the mighty deep and commingle seas and skies. These are some of the achievements of this agent upon the waters. At a subsequent period, we behold the iron-horse, whose feed is fire, outstripping the winds, as he glides over his mysterious foot-path and bids defiance to any competitor yet in existence. His neigh has waked up all the former solitudes of civilized lands, and created a universal stir among the people. He drags a hundred peace-chariots over the fruitful plains, along the river sides, on the edge of fearful precipices, over broad and navigable streams, and through deep ravines and mountain-passes. These are among the sublimer and more imposing achievements of this agent; but there are others, of humbler pretensions, which are not less honorable to the present age and not less profitable to man. We can only glance at these.

It cannot escape the notice of any one, that steam has already displaced many agents which have been employed, for ages, in the mechanical operations of our world. Horse-power and water-power have been both modified and diminished in their uses for the abridgment of human labor. This process is likely to go on to a still greater extent. Saw-mills, planing machines, flouring-mills, iron-works of various kinds, cotton-mills, printing presses, and a hundred other not less useful and necessary establishments, are dependent on this agent alone for their propelling power. In the construction of all kinds of machinery, and indeed in manufactures generally, it has become almost indispensable—so that its banishment from the civilized world would "bring again the shadow" on "the sun dial" of time, "ten degrees backward." This power, as it is now applied, is the great Anakim of mechanics; and whether it shall ever be surpassed in giant strength and giant speed, may depend on the successful results of some future electro-magnetic experiments. At any rate, we cannot go back. The aid of steam is now so associated with all our comforts, and so interwoven with all our executions, that we wonder how the world could have crept along, in a sort of snail-speed, for sixty centuries, without some impulse from its accelerating power.

But the achievements of science, in the application of its discoveries to useful purposes, are not confined to mechanical forces. Chemistry has done wonders in our day. While original research, successfully begun long ago, has been pushed into every department of nature, established results, more than formerly, have been made available in the practical business of life. Agriculture and the arts have derived new aids from this science, in our time, which have greatly changed the mode of many operations, simplified and facilitated many laborious and complicated processes, and made the culture of the soil and the products of the factory much more a matter of mind than formerly. Agriculture and manufactures may now be placed among the learned professions.

But the great achievement of our day is the electro-magnetic telegraph. This consists in the application of a known chemical agent to a new and valuable purpose. Nothing has been discovered but what was already a matter of science, and had been set down, "in extenso," in books ; but invention has here had her perfect work. It has been said that "FRANKLIN tamed the lightning." This he did when he drew down this subtle element from the skies and shut it up in a Leyden jar, or taught it to course harmlessly along the metallic rod, sparing our dwellings from conflagration and their inmates from instant death. But it remained for MORSE to give this etherial captive a good English education, and prepare him to become the ambassador of thought from man to man, annihilating both time and space in the execution of his office.

But I must not consume time by going into further detail. This is a practical age ; and one of its most marked and prominent features is, to convert knowledge to some use. Every learned profession—every branch of active business—every projected enterprise which spreads itself out in magnificence and grandeur and glory before the eyes of the world,—has felt the power of the feature of mind which prevails in our day. The very "fragments" of former thought are now carefully "gathered up" and put into modern "baskets," "that nothing be lost." These shall become the aliment of mind hereafter.

2. This is an age of increased *international communication.*

The position and feelings of the nations of our globe toward each other, are matters too well known to need many words on this occasion. Different portions of our race have been dissociated and repelled from each other, by causes almost numberless; and among these, language, religion, forms of government, social customs, national employments, ancestral stock or origin, degrees of barbarism and civilization, the color of the skin, ignorance of one another, ambition, fear and jealousy, and the memory or tradition of ancient feuds and wrongs, may be set down among the most prominent and powerful.

The original dispersion of our race, and their division into national organizations, after the deluge, was an act of God. It was effected by a miracle. At this period, there was one language and one people. They intended to continue one. For this purpose they began to build a central city and a magnificent tower; but God cut short their ambitious projects, because they stood in the way of his purpose, that man should "replenish the earth, and subdue it." This original design of Heaven could be brought about in no way more effectually, or more speedily, than it was by the confusion of tongues which God sent upon Babel. Besides, our race, in that period of the world, were not prepared to dwell together in fraternal bonds as one people, nor to maintain the more remote brotherhood of nations between different and sequestered portions of the globe. Nor must we forget, that the very animosities which immediately sprang up between different tribes and tongues, served at least one valuable purpose—that of cementing the bonds of union more closely among those who had common interests to protect, and who must provide for their common defence. They promoted home interests. Pressure from without consolidated the body politic within.

But another day has come; and one that "many prophets and righteous men have desired,"—a day in which the nations of the earth are becoming acquainted with one another. The dispension has answered its purpose, and God, in his providence, is bringing about still more beneficient results; and these are secured by that knowledge which attends the progress of the race. The world will now bear this intercommunication without neuteralizing her good by evil, or extinguishing her light in total darkness.—Among the intelligent and most active portions of mankind, civilization is entrenched in her strong holds, and christianity has thrust down her roots deep into the soil, and "sent out her boughs unto the sea and her branches unto the river."

The causes and the effects of an increased intercourse between the various nations of our globe, must be contemplated with great interest by the philosopher, the statesman, the philanthropist, and the christian. The fact of which I am speaking will not be denied. The age in which we live is making the world the subject of knowledge, and bringing its various portions together. Nations begin to study nations. We know more of India now than we did of continental Europe a few years ago. And our intercourse with the former now is greater than it was with the latter then.

The causes of this change may be easily discovered. They belong to our age. They are the natural and spontaneous developements of knowledge, ever accumulating from age to age, and assuming more and more a practical form,—of hoary-headed experience,—and of the more general diffusion of the word of God. Day-light is not more sure to follow the sun, than these effects are their causes.—Men have learned, at last, that a foreigner is not necessarily an enemy, that the best way to secure good from others is to do good to them, and that the reciprocation of kindness may exist between nations, as well as individuals. The world has learned more than formerly, though the lesson is not yet perfectly mastered, that the blessings of peace are above all price; and that wars, as they generally exist, with all their nodding plumes, and gorgeous epaulets, and shining buttons, and flashing blades, and golden hilts, and martial music, are only a fashionable mode of scarlet butchery,—and generally not less suicidal than murderous. This relic of barbarism will one day find its proper level. The holy scriptures which teach, that God "hath made of one blood all nations of men, for to dwell on all the face of the earth," have, in our day, produced in many minds a more kindly feeling towards universal man than has prevailed in ages gone by. The world begins to be looked upon as a theatre of benevolent, as well as commercial enterprise. Nations are now on speaking terms, and visiting terms. Nor do they address one another as they once did with the breath of fire and brimstone, and in the harsh accents of grape shot and cannon balls, and with the punctuation of sharp pointed swords and bayonets! This better spirit is partly the effect of increased international communication, and the same spirit is destined to multiply visits between the intelligent and good of every land, till all nations shall form one great family circle, extending round the globe.

The effects of this intercourse upon the present comforts, and the ultimate destinies of our world, can hardly be overrated. Intelligence, liberty, and the word of life, shall be scattered broad-cast in its pathway. Let the oppressed portions of our race, whether they groan under the exactions of kings or priests,—whether they are crushed down by the sceptered hand or the mitered head,—understand the condition of the people of this country, with our free press, our free gospel, and our free schools,—how long, think you, could the Grand Sultan of Turkey enforce his edicts, or the spiritual despotism of Italy brood, with raven wing, over the seven eternal hills, or the pseudo-republic of France wear its hypocritical guise ? The fact is, ignorance and tyranny seek obscurity and concealment. They fear the light. The late Pope of Rome was no fool,—what ever we may think of his viritable holiness now restored to the throne,—who refused to let a railway pass through his dominions. He knew that intelligence first kindled the fires of the locomotive, that a blaze of light attends his progress, and that sparks are often scattered along his track, which might set some materials in a flame that he, with all his holy water, could not easily extinguish.

The facilities for intercourse with all parts of the world, are such as the spirit of the age demands ; and these will be used more and more : and the effect of this intercourse, predicted by the prophet Daniel, shall be seen and felt the world over : "Many shall run to and fro, and knowledge shall be increased."

3. Our age is characterized by *the spirit of freedom.*

The noblest strife of man, is that war which he wages against moral evil ; and the highest freedom is that which

Jesus Christ bestows through the gospel. The christian warrior is a grand " spectacle to angels."

" Ask him indeed what trophies he has raised,
" Or what achievements of immortal fame
" He purposes, and he shall answer--None.
" His warfare is within. There unfatigued
" His fervant spirit labors. There he fights,
" And there obtains fresh triumphs o'er himself.
" And never withering wreaths, compared with which,
" The laurels that a Cæsar reaps are weeds."

Next to this, in the sublimity of its spirit, and in the length and breadth and compass and duration of its consequences, is the struggle for personal and national liberty.—God made man free,—tyrants alone make him a slave. It is not necessary, before the Anglo Saxon race, to enter into a formal defence of the principles of liberty, or to paint the deep curse of servitude. With us the love of the former and the abhorrence of the latter, are innate and living principles. They are a part of our being. They are our life-blood, the centre and mainspring of vitality. The following sentiments uttered by our own sages, will find a hearty and eloquent response from every American bosom. " Where liberty dwells, there is my country,"—" Sink or swim, live or die, survive or perish, I give my hand and heart to this vote,"—" Independence *now*, and INDEPENDENCE FOREVER,"—"Give me *liberty*, or give me *death*."

These sentiments which made our revolution, and lie at the basis of our government, have begun to produce their effects on mind almost every where ; and hence the fearful strifes of those antagonisms which have entered the field against each other, in our day. Every man should hail this conflict as an omen of good. Nothing is more to be dreaded than a dead calm where human rights are at stake. A people borne down by the exactions of a government which does little more than rob and pillage them, and making them a lawful prey, and who are, at the same time, regardless of their condition and their rights, are "twice dead, plucked up by the roots." Such, we have most of us supposed, *was* the condition of the greater part of the population of continental Europe. But recent events have taught us another lesson. We had examined the exterior of things only, while we had not studied the deep philosophy within. Mount Vesuvius is as quiet in ordinary times, as other mountains. but an underground process is going on, all the while; the lava factories are in full operation, the liquid mass accumulates, and rises higher and higher till the burning surface reaches the summit, and then all the imprisoned fires within find vent, and an ocean of flame consumes all that it meets in its progress. So it was in France, and so it was in Italy, and so it was in some parts of Germany. And so it will be again, at no distant period, in all these, and among other nations too. The people of most countries have too much light now to remain quiet under forms and administrations of government, which rob them of the essential attributes of humanity,—which repress the noble aspirings of thought,—which extinguish the kindling flame of independence,—and which strip the very body of its comforts to fatten and adorn the pride of the oppressor. Governments are designed for the good of the people, and they must all come to this at last. This is the true democratic principle. The conflict may be long, it certainly will be desperate; but I have no doubt, that the example of this country will yet give a free constitution to every nation in the civilized world, yea, to every people under the broad heavens.

Now is it possible, in such a day as this, when nations are brought into proximity with each other by steam-power, and the world is comprised in a nut-shell, and the people of different, and once far distant, lands, mingle like kindred streams, to keep any portion of mankind ignorant of what is going on among the remainder? Increased knowledge must be the effect, and that knowledge will produce changes which will modify old governments, or overturn them and give freedom to man. Liberty and human rights, voluntarily conceded, or *revolutions*, most fearful and portentious, must come; and let those who are most deeply concerned, prepare for the modification, or the catastrophy! The millions of Russia cannot always be crushed down by the paw of the Northern Bear: nor such a prince as employs and rewards such a tool as Haynau, have a place in the hearts of a generous people; nor such a tyranny as has despoiled the papal states of their ancient glory,—a tyranny deep, ponderous, crushing, abomniable, damning,—which has converted an Eden into a wilderness, the garden of the Lord into a desert, long stand amid the light and conflicts and glory of the present day. I would pray for peaceful reformations, and were I an actor in such scenes, I would labor for such ends; but if the CRASH must come, let it come, for God will be in it, and humanity shall be the gainer. Halleujahs shall be lifted up in heaven, when the last chain shall fall from the divine frame-work and the God-like spirit of man.

But we need not cross the Atlantic and visit the other continent, in order to witness the conflicts between freedom and oppression of which I am speaking. Never since the revolution, and, in some respects, not even then, has the spirit of liberty spoken out, in manly tones, as in our day Not that I would interfere with the institutious of the South. If they want slavery, let them have it. It is their own business, and not mine. But I have a right to think and say, that I believe it the deepest curse entailed upon the colonies by Great Britain, that it was most improvident and unfortunate, that the fathers of the Republic did not devise an early plan for its abolition; that, but for slavery, the South would have been the Eden of this continent, but she must now be supplanted by the great and free West; that as a government, we ought, for the love of God, and the love of country, and the love of man, to say to this blighting evil, "Hitherto shalt thou come, but no further; and here shall thy proud waves be stayed." This we may feel and say as northern men.

In relation to the Compromise, as it is called, I may be expected, in this connection, to say something. Take it all in all, I go for it. Let it not be disturbed, even by any modification, for the present. To be sure it contains some bitter pills, and they are not sugar-coated either! It is a little humiliating, that the United States—that is, we—have given Texas ten millions of dollars for a part of the lands which belonged to *ourselves* and not to *her*, and left in her hands *twenty-five thousand square miles* of our own territory, as a bribe or bonus, in order to make the ten millions go down with a better relish. But let Texas have it all, money and lands, for she is *poor;* and this settles the encroachments of slavery in our republic for ever. Call it a dower to our feeble young sister, if you please.

As to the Fugitive Slave Bill, I wish to speak plainly and advisedly, for I am aware that I speak with many eyes upon me, and many ears open to what I say. It is certain that the Constitution makes provision for the return from the Free States to the Slave States of *fugitives from service.* This Constitution is the only admitted bond of union between the States. Repudiate or nullify this, and the Union is broken up. While we continue one people, we must stand by this compact. We must observe good faith in carrying out its provisions, as a whole, and in all its parts. If one man, or one portion of the republic, may disregard or trample down one provision, another man, or another portion of the republic, may disregard or trample down another, and we shall have no Constitution left. The law in question aims to carry out a constitutional provision upon which the South have a right, by that instrument, to insist. I say nothing of the wisdom of making such a stipulation, but there it is ;—"it is so nominated in the bond,"—and we should keep it till we are prepared to surrender the whole system and break up the government. Whether the law is constitutional or not, I have had my doubts, as President FILLMORE had his, before he asked the opinion of the Attorney General ; and mine have continued even since I have read that opinion. But we have a tribunal to settle such questions, and the popular will is not that tribunal. It is the Supreme Court of the United States.

But whatever may be said of the constitutionality of the law, it is certainly very unfortunate and very ugly in many of its features. The process is altogether too summary—the investigation is purely *ex parte*, giving the arraigned not a moment to show who he is, or what he is ;—men are permitted, contrary to the first principles of jurisprudence, to swear property into their own hands ;—it erects an anomalous tribunal, and then offers a bribe to the judge by giving him twice the amount of fees for sending a man into slavery, that it does for pronouncing him free ;—and, if language means anything and is intelligible, it suspends the writ of "habeas corpus" where it could be of any use, when a man's liberty is at issue in the free State ; and if it permits him to use this writ at all, it is after he has been carried back into a slave State, where it would avail him just about as much as Popish masses would avail the soul of a poor sinner in making his escape from purgatory, if there were any such place. It might serve, as in the other case, to put money into professional pockets, but the poor victim would be left to grind in his prison-house, without hope.

But while these are my views of the law, I am sorry to see any portion of the North imitating that peevish sister of the South, who has always made more disturbance in the family circle than all the other members put together. But we should make some allowance for her,—for she inhabits a billious climate, and drinks in the beams of a fiery sun, and inherits a rickety constitution, which makes up the framework of her being—having a much larger proportion of *blacks* than of *whites*, and even this minor class must be put into two antagonistic categories: pauperism, and a self-styled aristocracy. But in the free, educated bone and muscle of the North, there is no excuse for nullification. We have been, and Heaven grant that we may continue to be, a law-abiding people. We have a Constitution, and we should preserve it inviolate, and carry out all its stipulations, in good faith, till we are prepared to 'tie a mill-stone around its neck and send it down to the bottom of the sea.' This ground I have always occupied. If we expect the protection of law, we must protect law, and see that its provisions are carried out. These were my views when General Jackson effectually rebuked the insurrectionary spirit of South Carolina; nor did I fail to express these same views when a majority of the General Assembly dismembered one of the largest and most efficient Churches on this continent, by cutting off sixty thousand communicants, without a trial, while they acknowledged that the proposition to do it was "unconstitutional and revolutionary." I quote the language of some of their prominent speakers, "*unconstitutional and revolutionary.*" And it is my glory, this day, that I am a "constitutional Presbyterian." And what I am in the Church, I am in the State.

I have one word more on this law. Let the South execute it, if they please, and let no one throw a straw in their way. But if it is executed, it will render slavery double-dyed in the deep popular execration of the free States, and especially if it be executed upon those who have long been in the enjoyment of the rights of humanity, and have families grown up around them. Or let the South take back the many thousands of fugitives who, they allege, are among us—many of whom are now intelligent and honorable men—and they would be so many torch-lights of freedom blazing, with prophetic rays, upon the dark midnight of slavery. The South better sacrifice ten times the amount of money at which they value these fugitives, than to admit such a corps of missionaries among them. If the North will keep still, and leave this law to itself and the South, all will be well in the end.

But I must allude to one point more. It appears marvellous to me, that while the members of Congress, North and South, are disposed to unite in carrying out the article of the Constitution for the return of *fugitives*, which has been evaded, as it is alleged, in the free States, other articles of the same great compact which are openly violated at the South, and that too under the sanction of State or municipal regulations, should not be thought of, or, at least, not provided for. The Constitution declares, that "the citizens of each State shall be entitled to all the privileges and immunities of citizens in the several States." And yet the free colored citizen of Massachusetts, regularly employed on board of a vessel belonging to that State, and his name entered according to the laws of the United States, is taken from that vessel when she enters the port of Charleston, South Carolina, and locked up in prison till the vessel departs. This is refusing citizenship to the person when the Constitution has given it to him. Besides, this imprisonment violates the fourth article of the "Amendments to the Constitution," which provides that "the right of the people to be secure in their *persons*, houses, papers and effects against unreasonable searches and *seizures*, shall not be violated." And yet there is nothing in the *Compromise* to carry out these articles of the national compact. When I have seen the great expounder of constitutional law —the second DANIEL—stand by the original compact, when Northern feeling and Northern prejudice were all against him, I have admired his magnanimity; but when I have seen this same champion insisting on the return of fugitive slaves, and leaving his own fellow-citizens uncared for in Southern prisons, I have said, with David, "*Lord, what is* MAN?" How easy it is to make the colored race scape-goats or sacrifices when cupidity or ambition may require it! This last remark should not be restricted to an individual.

4. This is an age in which *systems of religion are tested.* Every man should keep up with the moral and spiritual history of our world. He that does not know what is going on under the different forms and names of religion, must be ignorant of many things which go to make up a well finished mind. He cannot be a thoroughly educated man. To say nothing of the relations of this study to the panoply of the christian, it should form a part of the mental furniture of every intellectual and moral philosopher, of every political economist, and every man of literary and scientific leis-

ure. If other history is interesting, and often thrilling in its details, that of religion is much more so, for it embodies the doings both of God and man. And inquiries of this nature were never so exciting as they are in our day. Changes have been so sudden and so great, and some of them so unlooked for, that an air of novelty, and, not unfrequently of romance, seems to be thrown around them. We ought to thank God that we may witness these occurrences. "Many prophets and righteous men" would have done it, with acclamations which would have made the heavens vocal, if they had stood on the summit to which our feet have been conducted. They have prepared anthems for such occasions, though they were permitted to see these events only by the eye of faith, and as they were dimly sketched in prophetic vision; and yet we have little more to do in the expression of our thankfulness, than to sing over the songs which they have indited for us.

The last forty years have witnessed greater changes in the religious aspects of our world than have occurred during the whole period which has elapsed since the glorious reformation that commenced with Martin Luther. Many of the old religions of our world have become as a threadbare garment, and the people are disposed to cast them off, or "fold them up" and lay them aside. Look at *paganism* where it has come more particularly under our inspection, and you will see that it has had its day, and has nearly run its race. The Sandwich Islanders had tried a fair experiment with their gods, and finding from their own examination of the subject, that their whole system of worship was a mere human figment, they converted their deities into fuel for cooking their food. Since that period they have received the gospel, and under the instruction of missionaries, they have risen more rapidly in letters, and piety, and morals, than any other people of whom we have a minute and critical account. The transformation is almost miraculous. Go to the populous East, and the same facts will meet you on every side. Idolatry, though the national and popular religion,—and indeed the only religion they know,—is loosing its hold on the human mind. And this is often the case where missionary labors have either not been enjoyed at all, or have not been directly blessed in the conversion of men to Christ. Their false schemesof theology are wearing out and loosing their former attractions. In Calcutta alone, it may be estimated that from ten to fifteen thousand who were born and trained in paganism, have renounced that system, and may be said to be without any religion at all. The most ingenious, complicated, and magnificent schemes of idol-worship, which cover most of the eastern world, and embrace four or five hundred millions of devotees would be likely to die out for the want of inherent vitality, even if the gospel were to cease from its aggressive movements. The symptoms of that crisis, we are permitted to witness. They have supervened in our day.

Mohamedanism, too, has lost most of its ancient zeal, and its glory has departed, since it has had few or no opportunities of making converts upon the field of blood. Its days are nearly numbered, and its destiny is sealed on the earth, as it is in heaven.

But the greatest changes, in our day, have occurred in the papal world. They are such as many men, deeply read in the prophetic books, have anticipated, and have been looking for. They have now come. When I speak of the *papal world* I mean the church and state, for they are as vitally united as the Siamese twins: if one lives they both live,

—if one dies, the other dies also. I mean in their present organizations. The sceptered hand protects the mitred head, and the mitred head works out the problems of oppression for the sceptered hand to enforce. The causes of all the insurrectionary movements of France, Austria, Hungary and Rome, have been created as much by the church as the state. Indeed, without the papal power, Europe would never have worn the chains which have been rivited upon many parts of it, for ages past. This is especially true of the papal see. The people had been kept in ignorance, by a false gospel, administered by ghostly hands, and robbed of their dearest rights, till endurance was no longer a virtue. The struggle for a free constitution, in the land of the Romans, was one of the noblest that was ever undertaken, and failed of success among men. And had it not been for French troops and French bayonets, it would have achieved its object. And let it not be forgotten, that this war was waged against spiritual and political tyranny ; and Republican France fought for the tyrant.

The letter of that noble spirit Mazzini, late one of the Triumvirs of Rome, addressed to the Priests of Italy, reveals both the nature and the causes of the popular movements in that ill-fated land. I shall give you a few sentences from this masterly production.

"For a long time, a divorce has existed between the Catholic Church and humanity." "I now warn you that the important hour is about to strike. Through your misconduct—through your obstinacy in propping up a rotten edifice, and in maintaining the Popish church, notwithstanding its hatred to, and its ignorance of the inevitable progress of mankind—men's consciences are now in doubt. Religion is banished from men's hearts." "In the name of God, and for the love we bear our country, we ask you of what creed you are? Whether you understand the scriptures? Whether the word of Christ be to you a dead letter? Whether, in chosing between the word of God and the Bulls of the Pope, you be absolutely determined to stand by the latter without examination—without an appeal to your consciences? In a word, we ask you whether you be christians, or idolators?"

"What are the demands of the people? Nationality—Freedom—the general good of mankind; Liberty of speech and of conscience; protection of just laws, instead of the arbitrary caprice of a usurpation. We will select our own rulers from those most conspicuous for their virtues and intelligence. We will have education for all: Food for the mind—bread for the body; that the will of God be done on earth as it is in heaven."

Now these are American sentiments. We inhaled them with our earliest breathings; and we shall live by them and die by them; and then leave them as a legacy to other generations. And yet these sentiments were anathematized and banished by the present pope, his cardinals and priests. Yes, butcheries without number were perpetrated, by the aid of a foreign power, in order to drive them from the land. And notwithstanding this, we are told, in a late Lecture by Bishop Hughes that this country is yet to share the same fate, and come under the same despotic Prince and church. "Every body should know," says he, "that we have for our mission to convert the world,—including the inhabitants of the United States,—the people of the cities, and the people of the country, the officers of the navy and the marines, commanders of the army, the legislatures, the senate, the Cabinet, the President, and all." Nor, according to this modest arch-bishop, is this papal conquest to end here. "The object we hope to accomplish in time," says he, "is to convert all pagan nations, and all protestant nations, even England and her proud Parliament and Imperial Sovereign."

When I look at this pompous waste of words, in connection with what his papal master has lately done in Queen Victoria's dominions, dividing her kingdom into Romish jurisdictions, I am inclined to consider it all a mere "ruse" to divert attention from the state of things in Italy—from a tottering throne, from a beggarly and hated priesthood, from the only half-stifled demands of the people for the right of private judgment and political reform, from the successful distribution of Bibles and Tracts, and from daily efforts for the conversion of the subjects of his holiness, under the very shadow of St. Peter's. It is a mere 'whistle to keep the courage up.'

What! this country to become papal, and receive all the dogmas of the Romish Church! Will the American mind, accustomed to think for itself, and irradiated by human learning and the Bible, ever subscribe to her articles of faith and submit to *her* dictation in matters of religion? No, never, while the sun shines, and the sweet stars are in heaven. *Never*, while the earth is green, and Mercy is on the throne! We are not the people to swallow transubstantiation, the infallibility of the Pope, the right of the Church to supercede private judgment and the dictates of conscience, by imposing a creed that every man must believe, auricular confession, priestly absolution, extreme unction, prayers to a host of dead men and women, the doctrine of purgatory, masses for departed souls, the efficacy of penance and pilgrimages, and the puerile stories of modern miracles. But we ask no acts of Congress, or decrees of synods or conventions, to defend us from the predictions or the encroachments of the Bishop. This would be, as DANIEL WEBSTER said, in a far more doubtful case, "re-enacting the laws of God." Our shield is common sense and the Bible, both of which God has given us, and which neither Pope nor prelate shall ever take away. Let the Bishop vapor to his heart's content; it may gratify him—it will certainly do us no harm.

The case may be very different in England. I say nothing of Episcopacy here; but I do say, that the established Church of England was never thoroughly Protestant. A State religion, whether Lutheran, Episcopal or Presbyterian, has a fibre of Romanism in it, and especially if it have a temporal prince or potentate at its head. The English Reformation was partly, at least, a contest between the king of Italy and the king of England—the pope of Rome and pope Henry the VIII. The late defections from the Anglican church to the Roman Catholic, over which Bishop HUGHES glories so exultingly, and by which the Pope seems to have been moved as by a gentle invitation to come over and take possession of his own, confirm the position I have taken: that the Church establishment of England has always had a fibre of the root of the Papacy in it. I say nothing against an evangelical Protestant Episcopalian. I hail him as a brother. But to say nothing of those who have already arrived in Rome, I have no fellowship with that flank of the army which has wheeled towards the eternal city, are marching for the Vatican and Saint Peter's, and some of whom have travelled "as far as the Appii Forum and the Three Taverns." The rebuke administered to such, by Lord JOHN RUSSELL, is both timely and scorching. "Clergymen of our own Church," says his Lordship, "who have subscribed *the thirty-nine articles*, and acknowledged, in explicit terms, the Queen's supremacy, have been the most forward in leading their flocks, 'step by step, to the very verge of the precipice.'—The honor paid to saints, the claim of infallibility for the church, the superstitious use of the sign of the cross, the muttering of the liturgy, so as to disguise the language in which it is written, the recommendation of auricular confession, and the administration of penance and absolution---all these things are pointed out by clergymen of the Church of England as worthy of adoption."

"What, then, is the danger to be apprehended from a foreign prince of no greater power, compared to the danger within the gates, from the unworthy sons of the Church of England herself?"

There must be some deep-seated and latent cause for these frequent defections.

5. This is an age of *practical benevolence.*

Many of the facts and principles which I have already named, as belonging to this age, and forming the outlines of its character, have had a good practical effect upon the mind and heart and acts of men. This world, peopled with immortal beings, and these beings, our fellows, 'bone of our bones, and flesh of our flesh,' the subjects of suffering, crime, and death, has never before excited as deep an interest as now. I would not overdraw this picture, because I know the features I am delineating are but imperfectly developed as yet. We have only seen a few sparks, instead of the kindlings of the bright, warm fire. But that fire will burn in the human bosom, and much of the dross of our corrupt passions shall be consumed, and the pure gold of humanity and of grace shall flow in liquid streams from the furnace; and those streams shall enrich the world. It is not too much to anticipate that the time will come, when man will desire to live only to make the world smile around him,—to mittigate its woes and multiply its blessings.

Christianity is a scheme of heaven-born benificence. Its heart is love. If I had time I should like to present a faint sketch,—I *could* do no more,—of its deeds of mercy accomcomplished in our world. How, like its divine master, when enshrined in the soul of man,—another spirit within the spirit,—has it gone about doing good! I would point you to its monuments,—some of them moss-grown and hoary with age, and others in all the freshness of smiling infancy. I would tell you of its Hospitals, Poor-houses, Orphan Assylums, Widdows' houses, and Infirmaries for the aged and the indigent, with a hundred other homes for disease and want and wo, which have never grown upon the soil of our globe where it was not first watered by the dews of the gospel. But I forbear, because my object now is a different one. It is not to recount the victories of light and love, but to speak of the growing spirit of our day. Man begins to study man, not for the purpose of circumventing him—of robbing him—of making merchandize of him—of assassinating him, but that he may give him a frank and generous right hand, and press him to his warm heart, as a brother. This spirit is to set this world erect again, and lift its eye to Heaven, and chain its destinies to the throne of God.

The noblest expression of the spirit of which I am speaking, in modern times, may be seen in Christian missions.— The field is the world ; the object to be achieved is the redemption of immortal man. The agency is the Truth ; the efficiency is God the Spirit. Should not this be called a scheme of charity and beneficence ? Certainly it should be so called. By the side of it, most other enterprises are stripped of their grandeur and lose their interest. Others, after a temporary popularity, sink into neglect and are forgotten. But this, never. The Gospel has a mission to perform—a destiny to accomplish, which the good and active of all evangelical churches begin to believe and appreciate. This spirit already kindled, will become stronger, and more heavenly and Christ-like, in its pulsations and pantings for the earth's redemption. This world must be regenerated. God has so purposed. The inspired bards have thus sung, and the Church of God rests upon the promise. Hence the increased activities of all evangelical denominations in Christendom. There is a new spirit in redeemed man, and this spirit has created new and enlarged efforts for the redemption of universal man. It will never sleep again. It shall never grow faint or weary, till its purposed work is done. With God's help, it shall conquer every antagonism. Wars shall be known only in history. Sword-blades shall be plowshares, and sharp-pointed spears shall be pruning-hooks. The "*olive branch*," sweet emblem of peace, shall be held out from nation to nation, under the whole heavens, and the golden chain of brotherhood shall be thrown around the earth, and bind its peopled islands and continents together.

But this "consummation, so devoutly to be wished," can be secured only by the religion of mind—the religion of thought. Dogmas, taught by authority, and enforced by fire and fagot and inquisitorial tortures, can never make one heart better, nor fit one soul for Heaven. The Bible, the whole Bible, and nothing but the Bible, must be the system; and this must be administered in simplicity, and received in meekness and faith, and the work will be done. While stars shall sparkle in the crown of those who turn many to righteousness, the glory, both on earth and in heaven, shall be ascribed to God alone: and let all the people say, AMEN!

www.ingramcontent.com/pod-product-compliance
Lightning Source LLC
LaVergne TN
LVHW021200120826
845150LV00011B/2294

* 9 7 8 1 4 1 8 1 9 4 4 8 2 *